# The Ways of Grace

By

Audrey  Kharem, Ph.D.

The Ways of Grace
Published by Noble Strength Publishing
140 Roosevelt Ave, State College, PA 16801
Created 2018 by Audrey E. Kharem
Copyright © 2018 by Audrey E. Kharem

# Welcome to

# The Ways
# of
# Grace

## Preface

"The Ways of Grace" has been written in memory of my mother Grace A. Strong, born May 29, 1931. She transitioned from life to life on March 9, 2017. This book is not intended to be a biography. The scenarios included are solely based on my experiences with my mother coupled with my recollection of stories she shared with me about her life and some incidents that I personally observed or heard about from others. Certainly, family members and friends have had their own experiences with Grace and may have a different memory of some of the same events that I discuss in this book. With that in mind, I invite others to document their memories and add to the conversation in the space provided in Part 3 "Your Journey of Grace Journal". In the photo section, under some family members photos, you will see "DOB" - Date of Birth or "DOD"- Date of Death labeled, "unknown." That only means that the dates are unknown to me.

Although, I did feel that somehow I was appointed to fill the role of my mother's primary caregiver due to the timing of life circumstances, my unexpected early retirement, and her second breast cancer diagnosis., it is important to note that taking care of my mother was a joint effort. In addition to the professional healthcare staff, other family members and friends did what they could, as often as they could to lighten the load.

Before Mom's cancer diagnosis, she had monthly doctor's appointments to monitor the status of her other health issues. One of my sisters and I alternated from month to month taking Mom to the doctor. In fact, both times that I left the country for six to eight weeks, my sister stepped up and took over the full responsibility of our mother's care.

Shortly after taking on my new assignment, former colleagues commonly asked what I was doing now that I was retired, I'd always say that I worked for Grace Strong Incorporated. After giving them a few seconds to try to figure out what company that was, I'd smile, then tell them that Grace Strong is my mother and I have incorporated her life into mine. I always thought that was a clever answer.

Several years ago, two close family friends started calling Mom Grand-mom Gracie but I usually called her Gracie or Gracie-girl. She didn't seem to mind. Grace,

*Gracie, Gracie-girl and Grand-mom Gracie are all names that I may refer to in my reflections about my mom.*

*Grace was especially fond of her grandchildren and great-grandchildren and they were fond of her, too. My motivation for writing this book is to simply share a few Gracie stories that may be appreciated by others and support her loved ones with keeping her memory alive, for as long as they choose.*

## A Note from the Author

I hope that this book can provide some encouragement and a little comic relief for those who find themselves voluntarily or involuntarily in the caregiver role for a senior citizen. I also believe that this book can be a resource and offer a healthy outlet for readers who may be grieving a loss. Working through grief is a process that takes time and can be expressed in many forms including journaling. In Part 3, "Your Journal of Grace" there are pages with thought starters at the top followed by blank space to help with that process.

## Disclaimer

In this publication, you will not find a list of extensively researched findings regarding taking care of seniors, nor the best-claimed practices for how to maintain a work-life balance while caring for ailing aging loved ones. However, I have included a brief mention of common symptoms I observed while caring for my mom that's associated with aging, death and dying. In chapters

14,15 and 16 you'll also find general strategies related to caring for seniors that worked for me.

## Definitions of Grace

I am aware that when the word "grace" is mentioned, there are a variety of images or inferences that can come to mind, depending on one's life experiences. In my family, when someone says "grace", that always refers to saying a prayer before eating a meal—unless we were talking about my mom. Often, I hear the words "grace" and "mercy" used interchangeably as if they are synonymous. However, at Sunday school I was taught that "mercy" is when you are *not* given the negative consequences or response that you really *do deserve*. "Grace" is when you are freely given a positive response or consequence that you *do not deserve*, commonly referred to in many religious circles as "unmerited favor". Grace and mercy can also include divine intervention.

To verify if my childhood understanding of grace is still relevant, I decided to search for an updated definition. Here are a few of the results found for the meaning of "grace" from www.merriam-webester.com.

> 1a: unmerited divine assistance given humans for their regeneration or sanctification; b: a virtue coming from God; c: a state of sanctification enjoyed through divine assistance

> 2a: approval, favor; b: mercy pardon; c: a special favor: privilege; d: act of kindness, courtesy or clemency; e: a temporary exemption: reprieve.

Based on these definitions from the Merriam and Webster dictionary, it appears that my understanding of grace and mercy from my formative years is still relevant in this millennium.

As you read the following pages, my hope is that you are able to recognize the grace and mercy that have been present in your life and understand how significant my mother Grace's life and her memory are to me.

# Acknowledgments

Through this publication, I desire to shine a light of gratitude on the health care aides, nurses and social workers who provide direct services that support ailing seniors and their families. Being a caregiver for someone of any age with a chronic illness that results in limited physical and or cognitive ability, is overwhelming at times regardless of one's skill level, love, and loyalty. I sincerely salute my fellow family caregivers for what you are doing every day to sustain a decent quality of life for those in your care. A very special thank you to the team of healthcare professionals who graciously supported my family.

Thank you to all of the folks who helped shape how I experienced the ways of my mother, Grace. I am continually blessed when I consider all who helped me along this journey by your presence, prayers, words of encouragement, instructions, insight, laughs, companionship, listening ear or the provision of a ride or a meal. If

I failed to list your name, please charge it to my head and not my heart.

Thank you, Bobbie, Ricky, Juanita, Erica, Daniel, Kelli, Haroon, Sarah, Mitchell, Nasir, DJ, Adrian, Alanna-Lucylu, Malachi, Xavier, Khalil. The Brileys, Sameerah, Tymeer, Cal, Jeny, Chuantae, Lizzy, Keisha, Will, Stacey, Veronica, Stephanie, Amber, The MacKenzies, The Monachinos, Doreen, Sandra, Tony, Judy, Elisha, Kitzi, Arlene, Christal, Rodney, The Rannies, Donna, Sharon, Harriet, Sidney, Dr. Arenson, Norma, Cathy, Pam, Robin and Abdul. The Gill Street Ugroup, the Wednesday Night Encounter, the UCJC Intercessory Prayer team, the CCT Para-transit service, Pelham Pharmacy, Manna and the Megabus. A special thank you and a ton of gratitude to Gary and Lydia Abdullah for all of the personal time you have invested in this project as my proofreaders, editors, encouragers, and confidants. Above all, I thank God for his grace.

# Table of Contents

## Part 1

## Living With Grace

# TABLE OF CONTENTS (CONTINUED)

PART 1

*Living with Grace*

# one

## Raising Grace

Grace Altomese Huff Strong was born in
Philadelphia Pennsylvania on May 29th,1931. She
was the daughter of Gaddis and Ethel Huff.
According to her recollection, all of her relatives
before her, including both of her parents, were born
in the state of Georgia. She was the first person in
her mother's family to be born up north. On
Grace's fifth birthday, her mother Ethel died from
tuberculosis in 1936. After testing positive herself for
the disease, Grace was removed from her family

and placed in quarantine at the Rivercrest Orphanage in Phoenixville, Pennsylvania where she spent her elementary years. Being only five years old when this happened, she was very confused and felt abandoned. According to Mom, Rivercrest was run by strict Catholic nuns who were well-intended but not very compassionate. For example, although Gracie's hair was thin with a silky curly texture, the nuns claimed that they had no idea of what to do with a colored girl's hair, so instead of trying to style or braid it they just cut her hair off. Mom said she looked like a little boy and was often teased by the other children in the orphanage. She was one of only two black children living among approximately 60 white children.

The year she was discharged from Rivercrest, the United States was still fighting in World War II. Everyone's attention was on the war effort and many basic supplies were being rationed. I'm guessing, having another mouth to feed may have felt like "system overload" for struggling families. Perhaps that's why during the first two years after

Grace was discharged from the orphanage, she lived with a few different relatives for short periods of time, including her birth father. Eventually, she was taken in permanently by her mother's older sister, Aunt Alice and her husband Uncle Bobby, who became her parents. Mom told me that she lived with them until she ran away from home at age 17. Uncle Bobby did find her and tried to convince her to come back home. My Gracie-girl loved Uncle Bobby but she respectfully refused his request. She was ready to live life on her own terms and believed she had been granted the grace to survive.

# two

## Strong Grace

From what I observed from living with my mom, mixed with what she told me about her life, there appeared to be two ongoing themes in the back of her mind that motivated her to persevere even when life got tough: 1) work hard and 2) whenever there is a chance – play hard. As Mom described her life with Aunt Alice, her activities were confined to schoolwork and housework. There were chores from sun up to sun down. Whenever she was not in school, she was doing chores at home or working at someone else's home helping Aunt Alice do domestic work. On the other hand, as a teen, when she got a chance to hang out with friends, she'd risk the consequences of breaking curfew because she never knew when she would be allowed to hang out again. By the mid-1960's, Grace had been married, separated, divorced and was a single parent of four children. I suspect that her life could have been easier or at least less stressful if she had placed us in foster care, continuing the abandonment she felt as a child. Instead, she was determined to keep us. To say it was a challenging time would be a huge understatement. I chuckle to myself when I hear people say that they were poor as children but they didn't realize it until they were adults. That was not the case with us at all. We were living in poverty and felt every bit of it.

After my parents parted ways, I remember the five of us moving several times in the first year or so. We lived in each location for only a few months before we had to move again. At first, we stayed with our mom's sister then we moved to a one-bedroom apartment for a very brief time. I'm guessing that Gracie couldn't afford the rent for us to stay in the apartment any longer and make that place our permanent home. Fortunately, a lady from the church we were attending allowed us to live with her. I remember her house being full of things that I was not allowed to touch. I was a clumsy kid that seemed to break things just by standing too close. Though I was grateful to be there, being in that space full of fancy knick-knacks and large plants were stressful for me. Before we completely wore out our welcome, Mom was approved for an apartment in the Bartram Village low- income housing projects. Our new address was 2705 Ruby Terrace apartment 1B. When we moved into our new place we had no furniture or any other household goods that families need to turn a project apartment into a cozy home.

Material things didn't appear to be a priority to Gracie. Regardless of how hard it was, keeping us safe and fed with a secure roof over our heads, were

9

her only concerns. The first night we moved in, Mom dumped our bags of clothes on the bare living room floor, threw a sheet over the clothes and said: "that's your bed, now go to sleep". And we did.

Mom took full advantage of the educational and training opportunities that became available as a result of the 1960's civil rights victories. Shortly after attending the Leon Sullivan Opportunities Industrial Center, where she completed training as a clerk typist, she got hired to work in a typing pool at the Philadelphia City Hall Annex that was located in Center City near 13th and Market Street. In the sixties, it was a really big deal for a black woman to get a desk job working for the city. Especially considering that most of Gracie's former work experience only included waitressing, taking care of children and cleaning the homes of white folks with Aunt Alice.

In the early 70's, between jobs, she started a typing business in our apartment in her bedroom. Mom called her business "Little Grace's Typing

Service." Her customers were college students who needed someone who could properly format their research paper and give it a professionally finished look. Her typing skills spoke for themselves. The word about Gracie's typing business spread fast, and for a while, we had a variety of college students traipsing through our humble home on a regular basis.

Gracie later earned additional certifications in secretarial sciences and word processing. Her employment history includes the Philadelphia Quartermasters Depot, The Pennsylvania State University in the Office of Continuing Education, and The University of Pennsylvania hospital. She retired from full-time employment while working as an administrative assistant at the Philadelphia federal office of the Equal Employment Opportunity Commission.

Eventually, Mom did start having some fun. She enjoyed going to concerts, ballets, and the theater and became very active in her church. Since her goal was solely to enjoy the entertainment, she wasn't bothered by going out alone. When I asked her if she minds going to the theater by herself, she casually responded, "Well, yeah I'd like to have some company. But if I don't, I'm not going to let that stop me from having a good time."

During her later years, she accumulated a significant DVD movie collection, which served her well when she became homebound. Over time, Mom made friends with many of the neighbors that lived in her apartment building. Every Thursday night, she joined them in the community room for Bible study and every Friday night for game night. She admitted that sometimes they also played music and some of the residents would try to dance. When I asked her if she danced, she wouldn't give me a straight answer, only a smirk and said she had fun. Gracie also attended the programs coordinated by the resident managers. Just for the fellowship, she participated in programs that she didn't need. I remember finding on her kitchen table several brochures on how and when to properly test blood sugar levels and how to give yourself insulin.  I was totally baffled because my mother did not have diabetes.

Nothing made Gracie-girl happier than being with her family. Every year, she looked forward to having Christmas dinner with family members on her father's side. Every other summer she attended the family reunion with relatives on her mother's side. When possible, she went to the funerals of her family members and friends. When I accompanied her to these events, it seemed as if it didn't matter to her why we were there, she treated every gathering like a party. Coupled with her faith, spending time engaging with others is what kept Gracie strong.

# three

## Forgiving Grace

I believe forgiveness is one of the greatest gifts of grace that we can give each other and ourselves. Where there is forgiveness, there is hope. Hope energizes a fresh start that enables us to move forward and leave offenses behind.

In close relationships, regardless of how much people love each other, eventually there will be offenses – it's inevitable. My relationship with Gracie was no different. There were many offenses on both sides, especially while I was growing up. As a teenager, I thought my mother was too strict, too loud, overprotective and just bona fide crazy. Now that I am an adult, I believe what I use to think was Gracie's over the top crazy ways, was, in part, her way of keeping us safe.

Unfortunately, like many American cities, Philadelphia was going through a very tumultuous time in the 1960's and 70's. In addition to the fight for civil rights, there were race riots and gang wars throughout the city -- primarily, young men fighting over territory or turf. Innocent bystanders were often badly injured or killed as a direct result of being in the wrong place at the wrong time. At my high school, I remember violent brawls that involved police brutality in high gear, specifically aimed at African Americans. This was an extremely scary time for Black families. It felt as if black lives really didn't matter.

In contrast to other parts of the city, there was no gang violence in Bartram Village when we first moved there. Bartram Village was originally built in

1942 as homes primarily for white defense workers for World War II and their families. By the 60's, it was fairly integrated. There was even a maintenance crew that mowed the lawns in the summers and planted flowers in select areas in the spring. After a few years, as more Blacks moved in and white flight was in full effect, the amenities disappeared. Unlike some other housing projects, the Bartram Village apartment buildings were low-rise, only three stories high. Once, when I brought a friend home to meet my mom, he said our neighborhood wasn't a real housing project because the buildings were not like the high rises he grew up in, in New York City.

As I recall, it wasn't until the early 70's that gang activity began in "The Village". The location of Bartram Village in South West Philadelphia put its youth in a very vulnerable position. We were in between at least two active gangs. Just for sheer survival, some of the guys in our neighborhood formed a gang. So, in the spirit of protecting her children and keeping us in check, Gracie had strict rules that we were to follow.

First and foremost, when she came home from work, everyone had to be accounted for. Unless we had an afterschool job, we were expected to be in the house and no company. If we dared to let a friend hang out at our apartment after school, we were sure to put them out way before Gracie got home. Our homework should be done and the dinner was to be cooked properly and ready to serve when she walked through the door. No excuses. Of course, I was that kid who always had plenty of reasons for not completely following the rules. For instance, since we did not get an allowance and I didn't have a job, I had no money to buy the latest 45s. This "forced" me once to go next-door to listen to the new Jackson 5 hit record with my friend when I was supposed to be at home fixing dinner. At 13 years old, it did not occur to me that the rice, which I had left on the stove cooking, could burn (even though I left it on low heat) while I was happily singing along with the Jackson 5 and practicing the latest dance moves with my neighbor. When I finally burst through the door to check on the rice, it was too late. Gracie got home before I did. After throwing away the burnt rice she made sure I 'felt' the error of my ways and that I did not repeat it. Friday and Saturday night house parties were very popular when I was growing up. If I wasn't on punishment, usually I was allowed to go. No matter how far the party was or if I had transportation or not, my curfew was 12 o'clock midnight. No excuses. Most of the time, I made it.

Gracie grew up in a time when children were trained to be seen and not heard and sometimes not even seen. Like many parents, I'm sure her upbringing spilled over into her child-rearing practices. For example, Gracie considered it disrespectful for children to listen in on grown folks' conversations. We were not allowed to be in the same room with our mother when she was talking on the phone or if she was entertaining company, though that was rare. Whenever we addressed her, we always had to say "yes, ma'am" or "no, ma'am."

We had to be completely silent when she talked to us. According to Gracie's standards, interrupting her or any adult to get your point across was considered rude or giving backtalk, which was definitely a no-no. The most bizarre rules were the untold expectations about body language during a tongue-lashing. These rules were all learned through trial and error – mostly error. When she fussed, we had to stand up straight, no slouching or folding arms across the chest. We had to hold our head up but look down. I think staring directly into her eyes was considered a look of defiance. But don't look too pitiful, she didn't like that either. We could not roll our eyes or make heavy sighing noises while being reprimanded. For goodness sakes, do not laugh when she's being serious. Unfortunately, I had a nervous laugh that was difficult for me to control. It would bubble up at the most inappropriate times. But no worries – Gracie had the cure. When she gave me "the eye", the laughing would get stuck in my throat as I held my breath, waiting to get popped upside the head.

Years later, she often said that if she were parenting today, she would probably be arrested for child abuse because of her methods of discipline. Like many of the parents in my neighborhood, she firmly believed in corporal punishment when there was (what seem to her) an act of blatant disobedience. Typically, she fussed a lot while executing a beating. During the beating, she'd also ask questions that she really didn't want answers to – that was a little confusing. But what really frustrated me was after she beat me until I cried like a baby, she'd say "shut up before I give you something to cry about!" In my head I'd always thought (but never, ever said out loud) well lady, what do you think you just did?

Gracie's discipline tactics were quite predictable. But once, she did surprise me with how she decided to discipline my brother. At this particular time, we only had one telephone in our home. It was a black rotary phone attached to a wire that was so long that the phone could be carried into every room of the apartment with no problem. Soon after getting an upgrade in service from the Bell telephone company that included long-distance calling, my brother charged up what must have felt like an astronomical telephone bill to Mom, who was having a difficult time making ends meet. Gracie got so mad at him that she got quiet. I knew if Gracie got quiet she was really mad and that was not good. First there was angry mumbling followed by her quickly pacing the floor while squinting her eyes and sucking the insides of her jaws. What started off as quiet fussing gradually turned into Gracie cussing at the top of her lungs. When she acted like that, she reminded me of a volcanic explosion and that day, she really blew her top. This time instead of ending her rant with giving my brother the usual beat-down, she told him that he was not allowed to touch her phone, "don't even look at it until every penny of that phone bill is paid!" Then, for what felt like an eternity to me, Gracie made sure that he did not use, touch or look at her phone when she was not home. The only problem was, no one else had access to it either.

Every day she packed up the black rotary phone with the fifty-foot wire, in a brown paper bag and carried it to work until the long distance phone bill was completely paid off. My brother had a job after school and enjoyed spending his money on music and junk food. Gracie knew, making my teenage brother redirect his spending to paying the phone bill would teach him way more than getting a beating and it did. He rarely ever used the phone again after that.

Thankfully, maturity coupled with having a family of my own helped me understand two things that made forgiving my mother a lot easier. First, more often than not, even when there are two parents in the home, raising teenagers can be stressful. Second, my mother wasn't the only crazy-acting person in the house. During my teenage years, I challenged some of Mom's rules. I am certain that some of her crazy behavior was a reaction to my crazy misbehavior.

Overall, as an adult, I had a good relationship with Gracie. However, shortly after I became her primary caregiver, Mom and I got so mad at each other that we needed a third party to work through it. My sister intervened by separately encouraging Mom and me to think and consider each other's perspective, which really helped us come to a resolution. We were able to hear what the other was saying, release our anger, forgive and agree on a solution.

If forgiveness is going to be effective, it cannot be based purely on emotions. I believe forgiveness is an intentional, intellectual decision. Therefore, be aware it may take a little time for the emotions to line up with the decision to forgive. Yet, if we determine not to allow the negative effects of an offense to hold us hostage, we will reap the benefits of choosing to forgive.

One day, after getting home from a doctor's appointment, even before taking off her coat, Mom started walking slowly back and forth in the living room, then turned to me and said: "I'm sorry." I was puzzled. I had no idea what she was apologizing for. So I asked, "sorry for what?" She just said, "for everything. Everything I ever did that hurt you or hurt all y'all, I'm sorry." Though I was clueless about what specifically sparked her apology, I embraced it and said, "Mom, I forgive you" and I meant it. That brief intimate interaction between me and my Gracie-girl really strengthened our relationship. We moved forward not only as mother and daughter but as friends.

# four

## Walking with Grace

One of the last walks Mom and I took together is a walk that I will never forget. No matter the weather conditions, my Gracie-girl believed in getting outside every day and taking in the fresh air. When she couldn't get outside in the middle of winter she often opened her windows to let the fresh air blow in. When her walking became unsteady after the hip surgery, she was afraid to go outside alone. Mom often lamented during our phone conversations about being stuck in the house staring at the four walls. So when I came to town, my first assignment was to get her out of the apartment even if we just walked around the block, as we often did. To be clear, by this time a walk really meant her sitting and me pushing her in the wheelchair.

On this particular chilly fall day, when we left her building for an afternoon stroll, my only intention was to push Mom in the wheelchair around the block so she could experience the fresh air she craved. After leaving her parking lot, I noticed that the landscaping surrounding the parking lot across the street was very well kept. So instead of making a right turn and pushing her wheelchair toward the corner like I'd done so many times before, I asked Mom if she'd like to check out the parking lot across the street for a change of scenery. Her response was, "go for it!"

What I didn't know was that this scenic parking lot was slanted. Not long after I start pushing her chair, I realized we were quickly moving downhill. Honestly, the wheelchair almost got away from me a few times. As I struggled to maintain control of the chair I heard my Gracie-girl laughing and saying, "wheeee!!!" like she was enjoying a carnival ride at an amusement park. When we made it back up to the flat area at the entrance of the lot, I looked at Gracie and asked her how she felt. She had a big smile on her face and said, "do it again!" I'm sure our afternoon wheelchair walk looked very suspicious to passers-by. It was actually physically challenging for me to hold on to the chair going downhill and it was more challenging to push it back up. But it was well worth it to see her smile and hear my Gracie-girl laugh out loud. The memory of this walk with Grace brings me joy.

# five

## Trying Grace

Another nickname I called my mom was Gadget-girl. Gracie loved to try out new gadgets. Sometimes she ordered odd items from miscellaneous shopping catalogs just to see how they worked. For example, she always carried a tube of green lipstick in her purse. When I asked her about it, she put me at ease by first informing me that this lipstick is never green when she puts it on. She also let me know that this lipstick is special because it changes colors according to her body temperature. I guess her body temperature stayed the same because when she put on her special green lipstick it always looked pink to me.

Lipstick was really the only makeup that Mom consistently used but for some reason, she purchased a make-up apron. It looked like a giant silk bib trimmed in lace with three large pockets across the front. Her explanation for that purchase was that she just wanted to have it for whenever she decided she wanted to wear makeup. Then she turned to me and said, "I thought you might want to use it, too, so you don't mess up your clothes when you put your make-up on." Then she just stared at me wide-eyed for a minute like there was an underlying message that she wanted me to get.

Gracie especially liked trying out new technology when she got the chance. In addition to satisfying her curious nature, I believe this was also her effort to stay current as her she got older. In her words, she always wanted to know and be a part of "what's happnin." At one time, she had three cell

32

phones but didn't know how to work any of them.
But that did not stop her from daily clipping one to
her waistband or stuffing one in her pants pocket.
She wanted people to see that she was current with
the latest gadget trend like everyone else. When she
saw my daughter reading a book on her Kindle,
Gracie was determined that she had to have one.
She didn't know the name of the device. All she
could say was, "I want one of those things like she
has" as she pointed in my daughter's direction.
Knowing she wouldn't know the difference, I opted
to get her a Nook instead of the Kindle. With a
Nook we could always go to Barnes &Nobles to get
help as needed, as opposed to enduring the
frustration of downloading and interpreting
instructions from the Kindle website. Gadget-girl
Gracie was amazed at the Nooks' capabilities and
all of the information that was accessible via the
Internet. I set up an email account for her, which
she thought was very cool. But, she could never
open it unless I sat beside her and guided her step-
by-step. I think that little Nook became one of her

prized possessions. Despite never mastering how to operate it, she was proud of herself that she could keep it charged. In fact, the Nook stayed connected to the charger every day, around the clock. Except, when she was in another room, I'd unplug it because the wire would get hot. I was afraid the Nook was either going to combust into flames or take flight. I asked her why she left the Nook on the charger. She said in her a matter-of-fact tone, " I want to make sure it's ready for me whenever I'm ready to try it."

I believe one of Gracie's problems with modern technology was her lack of patience. I think she was stuck in a 1950's mindset, when televisions had fewer channel options and buttons to push, unlike what we have now. I remember in the 60's and 70's when our family's remedy for fixing a snowy screen was to give the television an open hand slap on the side. Or, it was common to turn the TV or radio off and on a few times to get it to stay on the chosen station. With that frame of mind as a reference, maybe that's why Gracie-girl's strategy was to just stand in front of her smart TV and frantically start pressing all of the buttons on the remote to get it to work. When she was completely frustrated, she would call me to let me know that she needs a new television because the one she has is broken.

After having the cable guy come numerous times to reprogram her television and remote control, at the advice of a friend I covered all of the buttons on the remote device except the power button and the up and down toggles for the channels and the volume, with two-inch wide silver masking tape. This method proved very effective for at least a year until she got curious about what was under the tape and removed it. We were back to square one. The same cable guy came so often that he gave me his personal number. Since it was an easy fix, he agreed to come to Mom's apartment as often as needed without charge to reset everything. This nice young man said he didn't mind helping Grandmom-Gracie because she reminded him of his grandmother who was always messing up her TV too.

Grace-girl was not what you'd call a fashionista but she was always interested in the latest fashion fads. Because of her curious nature, she wasn't shy about testing out new trends in clothing when she could get her hands on it. Once, I found a pink lace thong in her laundry. After recovering from shock, of course, I asked her about this panty surprise. In between both of us laughing hysterically, she said she ordered it from one of her catalogs because she just had to try it. She wanted to know what all the buzz was about regarding thongs. I asked her how she liked it. With a look of disdain, she said, "they can keep that mess! I don't want to be pulling a string out of my behind all day."

# six

## Saving Grace

From my early childhood, I remember Gracie being a fast walker. At her peak height, she was only 5 feet. She had short legs and small feet that matched her petite frame. Her walking stride wasn't very long but it was quick. Before power-walking was a popular thing, Gracie-girl was definitely into power-walking. I remember having to skip a little to keep up with her; even into my teenage years, she kept up a good pace.

Naturally, forty years later, walking with Gracie became a totally different experience. At the beginning of Mom's second breast cancer diagnosis in 2014, we used public transportation to go downtown for her doctor's appointments. I could tell she always put forth her best effort to keep up with the city foot traffic. In her estimation, she was still walking fast. But, I started calling her Speedy the Turtle because, though she was using a lot of energy, her pace was extremely slow. It was actually physically painful for me to walk as slow as she did, even when she used her walker. On several occasions, I swear I saw my life flash before my eyes when we were trying to make it across six lanes of traffic in Center City Philadelphia before our light turned red. Sometimes, I would have to firmly hold onto her arm and pull her a little bit to ensure we made it to the other side alive. When my mom would notice my anxiety, she always said, "don't worry – they're not going to hit us." But when I would see the oncoming, speeding traffic and hear the screeching brakes while trying to escape becoming road kill, my response was "Mom, we gotta hurry – these drivers don't even see us!"

After a few close calls, we agreed that our best course of action for traveling to and from doctor's appointments was to use the CCT para-transit system and her wheelchair. At first, she resisted by reminding me that she was still capable of walking. But, for the sake of our safety, I insisted on her using the wheelchair. Pushing a wheelchair is a lot less dangerous than trying to slow down city traffic with one hand like a school crossing guard without a whistle while pulling a senior citizen with the other.

# seven

## Black Grace

Grace was not a world traveler but when I was growing up, she talked a lot about wanting to go to Africa. She never identified a specific country in Africa she'd like to visit, just that she wanted to go there. I think she had a fantasy that the entire continent was a paradise free of racism and poverty and where black folks were in charge of everything and free to party all day and night. When we -- her children -- got on her nerves it was common for her to say, "if I didn't have y'all kids I could be partying

41

in Africa!" What I guess she didn't know is that in the Sixties, while African Americans were still fighting for civil rights in the United States, people of African descent around the world (including many African countries) were fighting for the same things: jobs, education, and fair housing.

During the 1930's and 1940's when my mom was growing up, African Americans were labeled Negro or colored. By the 1960s after James Brown encouraged us to "say it loud, I'm black and I'm proud," black became beautiful and African Americans proudly embraced the label Black, and Gracie was chief among them.

The 1960's were also the time when wearing an Afro first became a popular hairstyle for Black women. Grace-girl was determined to demonstrate her black pride and sport this popular hairstyle like many of her peers. The only problem was that her hair was silky with a mixture of stringy and curly strains that did not get nappy on its own. This meant that my sister or I had to tease her hair with a fine-toothed comb to give it a frizzy appearance, then use hairspray primarily marketed to white women to make Mom's hair stay in an Afro for a few days.

Demonstrating her Black solidarity, she brought home the Black Panther Paper every week, which she read from cover-to-cover and talked to us about the injustices that black people were experiencing in America. On Saturday mornings, while our friends were watching cartoons or doing their chores while listening to the latest R&B hits, we were doing our chores too -- but listening to music by Miriam Makeba and Hugh Masekela, who were both from South Africa. The funny thing is, Gracie loved being a Black woman but some people didn't believe she was Black, especially other Black people. As long as I can remember I have been questioned about my mom's nationality – even when she got older. Many of my friends thought that she or her parents were originally from India. As I alluded to earlier, Gracie was a petite lady. When I was a kid she weighed approximately

100lbs tops. Her hair was not extremely long but it was silky and shiny black. Before and after the Afro, she mostly wore a French braid down the back center of her head. I guess it was the combination of her hairstyle, those thick black eyebrows, the sharp, thin nose and olive skin tone that brought her racial identity into question. The only thing missing was the bindi, a red dot or gem on her forehead worn by many South Asian women. If she ever would've decided to wear a bindi and a sari she could have easily fit into a Hindu family photo without question. Once, when I told her that one of my friends asked if she was from India, she said, " I hope you told them no, that I'm black and poor just like the rest of y'all !"

# eight

## Growing with Grace

I am happy to report that over time my mother changed some of her staunch opinions and opened up to new ideas. I call that, "growing with grace." Believe it or not, initially, Gracie-girl was not in favor of me attending college. In fact, she sternly told my high school counselor to stop filling my head with pipe dreams. To get me to refocus on a career goal that she thought was more practical, at the beginning of my junior year of high school she made me withdraw from the college prep track and

45

enroll in the data processing and clerical administration program.

Holding firm to her position, during my senior year when I brought home the college financial aid application, she refused to look at it let alone sign it. Being poor does not exempt folks from having a lot of pride. Her argument was that she did not want "them" to know all of her business. At 17 years old I thought her reasoning was totally ridiculous, especially since I didn't know who "they" were or why she was so worried about "them" knowing that her economic status was below the poverty line. Since we lived in low-income housing and she was unemployed at the time, there's no way that our being poor wasn't already public knowledge. I took it upon myself to complete the Basic Education Opportunity Grant application. It was easy and quick to complete. The answers to all of the questions about family assets were the same – ZERO! My older sister forged Gracie's signature, for which I am forever grateful. With the grant money and scholarship awards, I had more than enough finances to start my college career. Realizing that there were no negative consequences to "them" knowing her business, Gracie was cooperative and fully onboard when my younger sister applied to college and requested her help with applying for financial aid.

Many years later, Mom told me that since she didn't have any money and I was not a straight "A" student, she didn't think earning a college degree was a realistic goal that I could achieve. She didn't want me to be set up for failure or get kicked out for not being able to pay tuition. When Mom's fear subsided she was quite supportive of me attending college. In fact, I think she could have been a great college recruiter. She started boldly asking young people if they were planning to pursue a college degree. If they hesitated or said no, she wanted to know why not — and further explained, "they'll give you some money if you want to go to college and you don't have to have all A's either!"

Gracie prided herself on keeping up with national events. She always said that it's important to know what's going on in the world. Every day, she read the newspaper and watched the morning, mid-day and evening news and the weather channel. However, when it came to the world of entertainment, for the most part, she stayed in her lane. Jazz legends like Ella Fitzgerald, Nancy Wilson, and Nina Simone always remained some of her favorite performers. She also enjoyed popular Motown artists like Smokey Robinson, the Supremes, Gladys Knight, the Four Tops and the Temptations to name a few. Pop music and rap were not on her radar at all. She told me that she didn't listen to that rap music because she couldn't understand what those kids were saying.

One afternoon, while I was coming in from the gym, Mom called out to me from her bedroom where she was watching TV. I could hear a little urgency in her voice, so I threw down my bag and ran to her bedside. She was engrossed in one of her daily talk shows. On this episode, for the very first time, Mom was introduced to singer and songwriter Usher. Little did I know I was walking into a teachable moment. This is how the conversation went:

> **Mom:** Have you seen this boy before? He can sing, got a decent voice too, but his name is Ushah.

> **Me:** Do you mean Usher?

> **Mom:** Yeah, that's what I said – Ushah!

> **Me:** Well, Mom he's been singing for a while now. He's also a good dancer, like Michael Jackson.

> **Mom:** All of that singing and dancing is fine but why does he have a name like Ushah? Is he an ushah? Did he ushah in church or the movies and people just start calling him Ushah? I ain't never heard of nothing like that! I was an ushah at Glory Baptist

Church and nobody ever called me Ushah, they called me Sistah Grace or Sistah Strong! Did his mother name him that? If she wanted to give him a name to feel good about himself, seem like to me she would've named him Captain or Major, something like that – not Ushah!

**Me:** Well Mom, I don't believe his mother gave him that name. His birth name is Raymond. I think Usher is a name he gave himself or maybe it was his agent or someone like that.

**Mom:** Hmph! (shaking her head slowly from side to side) He talks like he got good sense, I don't know why he would let someone call him that! But ain't nobody asked me so I guess I should keep quiet and if these kids like it I guess it's alright. From now on I'll just keep my mouth shut about that. But I had to ask if you knew because I ain't never heard of anybody wanting to be called Ushah.

**Me:** Well Mom, you are right about the kids liking him. That young man has made a lot of money writing songs, and performing with the name Usher.

**Mom:** Well alright then! If he's making a lot of money using that name, then Ushah is alright with me! Go 'head, Ushah!

# nine

## Thanksgiving Grace

I think Thanksgiving was my Gracie-girl's favorite holiday above all the others. It wasn't just eating an exceptionally good meal that she enjoyed, but it was also the fellowship, the planning and food preparation that got her excited. When we were growing up, I distinctly remember eating a lot of navy bean soup during the two weeks before Thanksgiving. I often wondered if that was intentional on Gracie's part to ensure we were thankful for Thanksgiving. Intentional or not, that strategy definitely worked on me.

For at least four or five years before Mom passed away we were blessed to get invited out to dinner for Thanksgiving. But that did not stop her from wanting to prepare her own specialty dishes at home including a turkey. She insisted that we needed to have our own Thanksgiving goodies and leftover food to nibble on when we came home.

In preparation for one of our last Thanksgivings together, Mom asked me to bring her a raw turkey from the area where I live. Her words were, "I know they got good country turkeys up there where you are. Bring me one to cook for Thanksgiving." Granted, State College is rural – especially compared to Philadelphia, but I don't live anywhere near a turkey farm that I'm aware of.

If I lived in the Philadelphia area, bringing Gracie a turkey would've been no problem, but the distance door-to-door from my home to hers was approximately 200 miles. Due to the frequent snow and icy roads during the winter months, driving can be treacherous, so I gladly took the five-hour ride on the Megabus. To travel around the city, I used public transportation, which was great, practical and convenient. The fact that I would be traveling on a bus didn't seem to matter to Gracie. For some reason she also seemed to not understand (although I kept telling her) that I don't live near a turkey farm and the grocery stores in Philadelphia carry the same turkey brands that they have in State College.

Unbeknownst to her, despite what I was saying, I was actually considering how I could honor Mom's request until I talked to my cousin. In her direct and humorous style, my cousin reminded me that a 12-pound turkey will not fit into my small overnight roller-bag along with my clothing, shoes, and toiletries. She said that I would look crazy carrying a turkey on my back stuffed inside my little backpack. Then she started firing questions at me like: how would I keep the turkey from thawing out for five hours on the heated Megabus? And, what will I tell the other passengers if my country turkey started to thaw and smell bad? And most important, how will I explain all of the mess to the bus driver and convince him to not put me and the country turkey off the bus in the middle of nowhere? My cousin's interrogation gave us both a good laugh, but it was also the reality check that I needed. I finally told Gracie flat-out that I will not be bringing her a country turkey from State College, but I was confident we would find one just as good, at a market in Philadelphia. When it was all said and done, I believe my Gracie-girl needed the turkey drama to help her be thankful, for the after-Thanksgiving meal.

# ten

## Cards of Grace

Often at our family reunions, relatives would stop and thank my mother for their birthday card. Once I overheard someone refer to her as the card lady. I know from personal experience that if I didn't get a birthday card from anyone else, I could always count on a card from my mother. When Gracie's mobility was limited and she was unable to get to the store herself, that did not deter her from her mission. Frequently, I was sent to the local convenience store to purchase birthday cards for friends and loved ones she wanted to acknowledge. To help her remember folks' birthdays, she had their birthdate written in her address book beside their name, telephone number, and address. She also kept a supply of stamps on hand, so she could be certain to get the cards in the mail in time for the person to receive it reasonably close to, if not on their actual birthday.

When I asked her why she was so committed to sending out birthday cards, she responded, "It ain't no big thing. I can't afford to buy everybody I love a present, but I can give them a card. I think everybody should get at least one card for their birthday and I think they like it. And, I like doing it, but it really ain't no big thing."

When I experienced my first birthday without receiving a card from Gracie, I really missed it. For me, it was a big thing. It is amazing how a simple birthday card can go a long way to make a person's day. Small acts of kindness really do matter.

# eleven

## Finding Grace

In addition to going to doctors' appointments, going to the market was our other regular outing. When Mom had the energy and before we started using the wheelchair, we would take the train and go shopping at the huge farmer's market in Center City Philadelphia at 11th and Market Street known as the Reading Terminal. Gracie did not believe in buying a prepackaged bag of fruit or vegetables. She was old-school, which meant she had to personally hand-pick and closely inspect each piece of fruit and every vegetable before it was dropped in her basket. Prior to our arrival, she always reminded me that she wanted to leave the Reading Terminal before five o'clock. She did not want to risk not being able to get a good seat (close to the door) because of the train getting crowded with the after-work commuters. However, once she started her veggie and fruit inspections, she seemed to be in a trance and lost all concerns about the time and train schedule. At the end of the day, it really didn't matter because someone was always kind and graciously insisted on giving her their seat if the train was full. I was the one that was left standing while holding fifteen pounds of prized produce.

Going to the market remained one of our regular activities even as Mom's symptoms progressed. Instead of going into Center City, we went to markets in her neighborhood. I used to think that going to buy groceries was a low-key, uneventful activity. But I learned that the hours between one and three in the afternoon are actually senior citizen shopping hours at the Ridge Avenue Shoprite. It was truly eye-opening to experience how shopping for groceries with senior citizens can be hazardous. Just imagine a dozen senior citizens moving around a parking lot, appearing to be totally unaware of each other. Some are attempting to park big cars while barely seeing over the steering wheel and others appear to be aimlessly pushing their shopping carts to who knows where. Getting inside the store unscathed during senior hours was an adventure.

In my effort to not add to the Shoprite drama, I always asked my mom before we left the apartment if she needed anything to eat and if she needed to use the restroom. Her answer was always, "I'm fine." So on a sunny fall day, with Gracie being "fine" and me armed with the grocery list, I felt secure that I was prepared for our afternoon grocery shopping outing. Since I could not push a shopping cart and a wheelchair at the same time and putting Mom in one of those motorized combination wheelchair-shopping carts was totally out of the question, we decided that she could use her walker while I pushed the shopping cart. Letting her out of the car right in front of the store deterred Mom from wandering around the parking lot, so that's what I did. As I watched her walk into the Shoprite, I felt good because that part of our plan worked out perfect.

Not long after scanning the produce section, (which is the first visible area when you enter the store) Mom announces that she is hungry. I'm not sure if it was the ten-minute ride from her apartment to the market that stirred up her appetite or the sight of all the aisles of food. But she insisted that she was near starving and needed a hot meal. I thought to myself, "okay, no problem – I'm in a store full of food. I can probably even pick up a few of the groceries on the list on my way to getting her something to eat." Unfortunately, most of the pre-fixed entrées available for purchase were cold meals, which I knew would not work for her. So I went back to the produce section where I left her to tell her the news but she was not there. She was not there! I was suddenly thrown into panic mode like a young mother who just lost her three-year-old at the mall. Before I knew it, I was quickly pushing my shopping cart up and down the aisles, checking out every little old lady that crossed my path while being careful not to run them over. Then I had a very scary thought that "maybe she left the store." Then came my repeated prayer, "Please God – NOT the parking lot! Please, God – not the PARKING LOT! Oh Lord, don't let her BE – in the parking lot !" I think I said that twenty times while I darted out the door to scan the area. My prayer was answered, she was not in the parking lot, but that realization did not ease my anxiety. Running full-speed back into the store, I landed in the produce section where we started and voilà! There she was. I couldn't believe my eyes. I was so relieved I almost cried. Seeing that I was totally stressed out, Mom calmly asked me what was wrong. Once I caught my breath, I explained how I've been looking for her all over the store and even went outside to check the parking lot. Her response nearly blew me away. She cocked her head to the side and said, "I saw you going up and down the aisles. I wondered what you were doing since you weren't picking up any groceries. Oh well, I'm glad you found me. But, did you get me anything to eat? Because, you know, I'm still hungry."

# twelve

## Good Looking Grace

As far back as I can remember, my mother was always struggling and stressed out, but she was still an attractive little lady. Years ago, when she walked down the street past a crowd of men, it was common for her to get compliments and catcalls. From Mom's stoic facial expression I could never tell if her response was a look of total annoyance or if she was shy, or just being modest in front of her children. She simply kept her gaze straight ahead, focused on wherever we were going and appeared not to hear the men yelling, trying to get her attention.

Fast-forward several decades when the male hospice social worker came to Mom's apartment for our intake consultation. This time I witnessed another side of my Gracie-girl. The day before the home visit I told her several times that the social worker would be coming and it was her choice if she wanted to meet with us or not. I was sure to mention his name so she knew that our social worker was a man. You see, once while recuperating in the hospital from a serious fall, she became very uncooperative when she learned that a male nurse had been assigned to take care of her. Needless to say, I had to inform the hospital staff and insist that only female nurses are to care for my Gracie- girl. As you can imagine, I was relieved that having a male social worker didn't matter to her at all. The following morning, before the social worker was scheduled to arrive, she still wasn't interested in participating in the intake appointment. In fact, she did not shower, get dressed or do any of her usual morning rituals. She chose to stay in her bedroom with the door closed and watch television.

When the social worker came in, he and I exchanged pleasantries and got busy completing the required paperwork, with my sister participating as well by speakerphone. Towards the end of our appointment, he asked if he could meet our mother because she really was the true client. So he could make her acquaintance, I went into the bedroom and asked her to come out and join us. I'm not sure who she expected to see but her body language and facial expression let me know that she was very happy when she saw the young ebony gentleman sitting at her kitchen table. She paused and looked him up-and-down with a big grin on her face. The social worker started out by giving her a handshake, stating his name and asking her some basic questions which Gracie-girl ignored. He asked how she was feeling and if she could tell him a few things about herself like what she enjoyed doing, what her favorite TV shows were, and the type of music she liked to listen to. She just stood there smiling at the young man for quite a while and then answered his questions with a response that floored me. As she slowly walked to stand directly in front of him with her hands on her hips, she said "I don't know nothing about all of that right now. What I do know is that you're a good-looking man!" I didn't say anything out loud, but in my head, I was thinking; "alrighty Gracie-girl, you may be sick, but you still know what looks good to you, and you don't have a problem saying so. Lord have mercy !"

# thirteen

## High Grace

What I dislike most about breast cancer is, as it metastasizes into the bones, it does not go about its business quietly. Instead, cancer makes its unmistakable presence known by inflicting tremendous pain as it breaks down the body's capabilities and confiscates its strength. As the disease progresses, so does the pain. As the pain increases, so does the strength of medications, especially in the late stages of cancer. In traditional medicine, the only arsenal that most doctors have to combat the pain is to prescribe strong narcotics to help patients cope and achieve some level of comfort. The downside of this for Gracie (and others, I'm sure) is, as the medication gets stronger, the level of comfort is maintained but the level of cognitive ability significantly decreases. I was told by one of the nurses that typically with breast cancer, the journey of decline goes from the breast to the bones then to the brain. Sixteen years prior to the second bout with breast cancer, she was diagnosed with hepatitis C. Hepatitis C also affects cognition in seniors which definitely complicates matters.

My mother's breast cancer symptoms followed the textbook description. In addition, Gracie also had high blood pressure, which seemed to go up when the pain increased. Knowing all of this, my sister and I (being dutiful daughters) devised a plan to help Mom stay on track with her medication. She was armed with a large pillbox for every day of the week; that had four color-coded labeled compartments: morning red, noon yellow, evening green, bedtime blue. She had a wonderful local pharmacist as a part of the care team. To ensure that her medications were always available in the correct doses, one of the pharmacist's assistants came every Thursday morning to Gracie's apartment to get her pillbox for the pharmacist to refill. To make sure that she did not miss taking a dose of her meds for that day, she was given a smaller pillbox with a one-day supply of everything. Later that same evening the pharmacist's assistant returned with the big, colorful pillbox refilled for another week.

Fentanyl is a narcotic that was prescribed to Gracie for the pain. It was not a pill that could be placed in the box. It was a small patch that she had to remember to change every three days on her own. To help with this process, I put a large calendar on her wall in the kitchen where I or my sister indicated when to change the patch. In fact, on the calendar on every third day, we wrote in large capital letters, "CHANGE PATCH." In addition, we took turns calling Mom to remind her to take her pills or change the patch if it was the third day. Gracie often complained about having to take so many pills but she was still compliant and followed the calendar pretty well – or so we thought.

Well, about two months after we incorporated this strategy, I start getting calls from the pharmacist expressing concern that Grandmom-Gracie may not be taking all of her pills every day, despite what she was telling us during our daily phone check-ins. This was followed by reports of strange behavior totally uncharacteristic of Gracie. I received word that she'd been walking the halls of her apartment building late at night when she should be sleeping. Her neighbors claimed that she let a strange man into her apartment, and one day, she was in the hallway yelling that she was hungry but had a refrigerator full of food.

After a bit of investigation, we realized what was going on. Our dear mother was choosing not to take her blood pressure pills and putting on too many of the fentanyl patches. In other words, my Gracie-girl was high as a kite! Intoxicated and disoriented from pain patches and elevated blood pressure! It's scary to think that she could have caused her own early demise. I am forever grateful for the grace of God from on high for sparing my mom Grace.

# fourteen

## Changing Grace

I think the elders in my family maintain a youthful appearance for quite some time as they advance in years. People were often surprised when they learned Gracie's age during her latter years before she got sick. Nevertheless, if we live long enough, signs of aging do catch up with us all.

Watching my Gracie-girl age gracefully over time is what I expected. However, as the invading diseases robbed her of her appetite, she became physically weak and her appearance start looking different. But, what stays with me, even more, are the unexpected behavioral changes. In addition to the breast cancer getting worse, the hepatitis C began to take a toll. Both of these ailments can affect the brain and disrupt the normal thought processes, particularly in seniors. The doctors and nurses warned me that there would be a decline in Mom's cognition similar to that of patients diagnosed with Alzheimer's disease.

To help me understand the changes in her behavior, I started reading various articles on the Internet about dementia, Alzheimer's and the body's transition from life to death. I also picked up a copy of the book by B. Smith and her husband, Dan Gasby titled "Before I Forget." This book was a wonderful resource for explaining in laymen terms, common behaviors exhibited by people with Alzheimer's. Some of these symptoms I knew nothing about before caring for my mom and reading this book.

For instance, rummaging is a symptom seen in many patients with Alzheimer's. Rummaging is described by Gasby as repetitive sorting through one's belongings as if they are looking for something but never finding it. While Gracie-girl was rummaging, she always forgot what she was looking for and would leave a big mess in the middle of the floor. This behavior really agitated her nurse's aide. I'm sure the young lady did not appreciate picking up the same large pile of Mom's stuff every day, but more importantly, there was a genuine concern for her safety. After rummaging, Gracie would leave a huge pile of her belongings on the floor right in the path between her bed and the bathroom. The aide and I knew that this rummaging situation was creating a trip-and-fall accident that was bound to happen if I didn't do something. To resolve this problem, I convinced Mom to let me pack her belongings in boxes and put the boxes in her closet. She agreed. I put a note on top of each box that said: "do not touch." To my surprise, that worked!

Sun-downing is another common symptom of Alzheimer's that I became familiar with. Out of all of the symptoms that caused a change in Gracie-girl's behavior, sun-downing is the one that caught me off-guard the most. According to WebMD, sun-downing affects individuals with Alzheimer's disease and other forms of dementia. Typically sun-downing symptoms begin in the late afternoon or early evening as light begins to fade. Individuals experiencing sun-downing may become suspicious, demanding or disoriented, and symptoms can worsen later in the evening. With my Gracie-girl this only happened once that I'm aware of, but once was enough. It was approximately four o'clock and the hospice nurse had come for her routine visit. The nurse and I were pleased that Gracie's heart rate and blood pressure were stable and overall she had a good check-up. From the outset, Mom seemed to really like this nurse; there was always a lot of talking and laughing when she came. On this particular afternoon, as soon as the nurse left the apartment, Mom's facial expression changed. I thought, maybe she was sad because the nurse had to leave. When I asked Mom if she needed anything, she responded in a tone that I did not recognize. I walked closer to her and asked the question again. This time, her voice and words were filled with suspicious hostility. She proceeded to tell me that she doesn't want me to get anything for her, then asked me why was I in her apartment. She wanted to know what was my name and where did I come from? At first, I actually thought she was joking. However, the tense expression that remained on her face let me know that this was no joke. When she told me to get out of her apartment and don't come back, I knew I was dealing with a serious situation. Thankfully, I was able to reach the hospice nurse immediately and she explained the sun-downing syndrome. She also instructed me to give Mom a dose of her detoxifying liver medicine and have her lay down for a little while. One hour later when it was completely dark outside, I checked on my Gracie-girl and she was back to her old self. From that day on, I made a habit of turning on the lights and closing the blinds well before sunset. This way, the atmosphere in the apartment was constant regardless of what was happening outside.

In addition to not recognizing familiar faces, some people with dementia symptoms don't always recognize their personal belongings. Mom went from rummaging and behaving like a hoarder to not recognizing some of her most common and valued possessions.

While Mom could still safely use her walker, she enjoyed going to the Thursday night Bible study held in the community room of her apartment building. As part of her outfit one Thursday evening, she wanted to wear one of her many suit jackets. I asked her to pick out the one she wanted to wear. When I tried to help her put on the jacket she selected, she refused, insisting that it was not hers. I thought I had been transported to the Twilight Zone. Gracie and I went back-and-forth several times, with me saying "Mom, this is your jacket" and she saying "no, it is not my jacket."

Getting nowhere, I asked her to pick out another jacket. When I attempted to help her put it on, the whole bizarre verbal exchange started all over again. Finally, I suggested that she borrow the jacket for the evening and when she comes back from Bible study, she can return it. She was satisfied with that arrangement. I thought we were in the clear until I tried to give her her Bible. She refused that too, again claiming that it was not hers. I knew my mom had had that same Bible for at least forty years. Rather than argue with her this time, I quickly suggested that she borrow that, too. She was okay then and happily went to her weekly Bible study.

In the literature on the cognitive decline of seniors, there is a lot of discussion on repetitive behaviors. I was used to Mom repeating the same stories over and over again, so I thought that was the extent of the repetitiveness until one morning when she called for my help.

At this time, Mom could still independently take care of most of her personal needs. Gracie's morning routine involved her going into the bathroom alone, taking a shower, putting on her disposable underwear by herself, then getting dressed for the day. One morning, it felt like she was taking longer than usual but I thought maybe she was just moving slower until she yelled my name. Immediately, I felt the adrenalin rising and ricocheting through my body. I ran to the bathroom, fearful that my mom had fallen down in the shower. To my surprise (and amusement), she was standing by the toilet holding on to the safety railing wearing six or seven pairs of disposable underwear. This was a hysterical sight. Some pairs were wrapped around one leg or an ankle and a few pairs made it up to her waist. I was relieved when she started laughing too. I was laughing so hard as I freed her from the tangle of underwear that tears were streaming down my face. All she could say was, "I don't know what happened," and I didn't ask.

# fifteen

## Embracing Grace

When you're immersed in the care and management of another person's life, it can become all-consuming. Even when you are not in their presence, concerns regarding their welfare stay on your mind 24/7; at least, that is what happened to me. As a result, it didn't take long for me to realize that I needed to be intentional about taking care of myself. I learned to drop my pride and embrace the acts of kindness that were offered time and time again. So when the hospice care team suggested an at-home care plan that included the support of respite care so I could take three-hour breaks every day away from Mom's apartment, I accepted. Admittedly, Mom and I were skeptical at first. We were not accustomed to strangers being in her apartment for long periods of time or cooking her meals and tending to her personal needs without me being there. Fortunately, the nurse's aides that came to my rescue were caring, professional young women, who quickly put me at ease. It was not so easy for Gracie. She had always been a very private and independent person.

I recall when the cancer mass was first discovered in her right breast, we were told by the oncologist that it had metastasized to Mom's right hip and she needed to have hip replacement surgery immediately. During her recovery, a lovely, soft-spoken woman was assigned to be Mom's personal-care aide at home. By the third visit, things seemed to be going well, so I left Mom in the hands of the aide while I walked to the convenience store only three blocks away. When I got back, the personal-care aide was gone. As soon as I walked through the door, Mom informed me in a loud stern voice, that she had fired the aide. Her exact words were, "I told that woman that she needs to go home and don't come back here no more! I don't need no help taking a shower!" In all fairness to my Gracie-girl, I did warn the aide to just station herself close by the bathroom door to make sure my mom was safe, but do not try to help her bathe. Instead, she could assist Gracie with something less intrusive, like putting lotion on her back or her feet. I'll never know for sure what took place while I was at the store. I only know what my Gracie-girl told me and that I never saw that personal-care aide again.

During the latter months of her illness, Mom stopped resisting the idea of an aide once she understood that they were there for my benefit as much as hers. Being a caregiver for a loved one with a terminal illness requires time, energy and a personal commitment beyond what most people anticipate. Accepting help from social service agencies, family members, neighbors, and friends is a demonstration of "grace" for the patient and the caregiver.

Maintaining Mom's weight was one of the goals of her home health care plan. The nutritionist encouraged Mom to eat plenty of carbs. She ate cake, cookies and other pastries along with bowls of ice cream and milkshakes in between meals. That was perfect for her since she had a sweet tooth but a sugar-and-carbohydrate laden diet would be a disaster for me. It is common knowledge that stress often causes people to eat too much, especially of the wrong things or not eat enough of anything. I made sure there were always fruits and vegetables on hand and enough bottled water in the refrigerator for both Mom and me. Proper nutrition for caregivers plays a vital role in keeping stress levels down.

Exercise is important too. Working out at the gym and taking long walks in Mom's neighborhood became part of my daily schedule, rain or shine. In addition to getting good physical exercise, these activities were rejuvenating for my soul.

Every day, Mom and I had a lot of conversations usually about whatever was on TV, unless she was in the mood to tell me again a story about her upbringing. When she could no longer talk to me, I still talked to her, but it was equally important for me to talk to other people, too. Conversing with others who were familiar with my caregiver role was affirming. However, it was refreshing to also talk to folks who had no idea how I spent my days or that my mom was sick. Usually, these talks were with total strangers who offered a completely different yet very interesting conversation.

There is a ton of information available in books and on the Internet that outlines the importance of self-care for caregivers. In the spirit of my Gracie-girl, I'd only add, when God sends help, take it. Don't look a gift horse in the mouth, just say thank you.

# sixteen

## More Grace

As I've already implied, the primary caregiver role usually involves much more than escorting a loved one to doctor appointments. Experience has taught me that the additional tasks also require an extra measure of grace, especially the financial management responsibilities. If an ailing senior is forthcoming with the documents outlining their financial status, and they've made their final wishes known for their after-life care, the easier the job will be. Otherwise, the lack of information can wreak havoc and confusion for the family.

Fortunately, I was able to get copies of Mom's "papers" while she was still quite lucid. In other words, I had a copy of her life insurance policy, Social Security card, Medicare card, and other health insurance information, in addition to being a joint owner on her bank accounts. I also had power of attorney and was the executor of her estate. Knowing Gracie's personal preferences also made some decisions very simple. For instance, she told me on several occasions that she never wanted to be placed in a nursing home. So I knew when her doctor suggested hospice care, it would be an in-home service for sure.

That part was easy in comparison to getting Gracie-girl to discuss her final wishes. Talking to her about anything related to death and dying was as taboo as talking to her about sex. However, a long time ago she did tell me that she definitely did not want to be cremated. I think she thought that was ungodly. It's funny, as much as she loved the Lord and going to church, I never heard her talk about looking forward to going to Heaven, that's probably because she knew she'd have to die to get there. Instead, Gracie frequently said that she wanted to live to be one hundred.

It takes longer to figure out the benefits and boundaries of a loved one's healthcare and after-life care plan, without access to their insurance policies. This is critical, because the level of resources determines the level of care, in life and in death.

Anyone who has ever been in the caregiver role will certainly agree, that it lessens the stress to have an idea of what information is most helpful to know. Here are a few things that I found to be essential:

- **Get the papers!** If at all possible, get copies of your loved one's insurance policies, bank statements, bills, the will, and Social Security number. All of this will prove helpful in the long run. I knew that, as a retiree, Gracie's primary income was from her Social Security. However, when carefully scanning her bank statement, I learned that she also got a small pension that had been automatically deposited monthly into her checking account. As executor of her estate, it was my responsibility to call her former employer to inform them of her death and formally request a stop payment of her pension. Otherwise, I would be liable for those funds and be required to repay them once they learned Mom was deceased.

**- Know what type of medical support is covered by your loved ones insurance.** It's good to have an understanding of how Medicare and other assets factor into the equation. After one falling incident, the medical care team suggested to my sister and me to place Gracie in a nursing home facility for a short stay until she was reasonably stable. Knowing that Gracie did not want to ever be in a nursing home, coupled with learning that her insurance would only partially pay for it and any other assets she had would have to be relinquished to guarantee payment, made it easy to reject that suggestion.

**- Investigate social service agencies in your area that provide assistance of some sort, to seniors.** In Mom's neighborhood, there's an agency called Center in the Park and the building is actually located in a park. This agency provides a variety of programs for senior citizens including computer classes, afternoon movies, line dancing, free meals and bus excursions. For a short while they scheduled and paid for Mom's para-transit rides to and from the doctor appointments as well as arranged for her to receive Meals on Wheels. In the city of Philadelphia, there's an agency called the Philadelphia Corporation for Aging (PCA). It is like a warehouse of resource information for senior citizens regardless of their physical condition. Through PCA each client is assigned a social worker to help identify the most appropriate services. My guess is that there are similar agencies in most other cities throughout the U.S.

**-Utilize all of the members of your loved one's care team.** In addition to the oncologist and the primary care physician, there was a nutritionist and a social worker as a part of Gracie's hospital care team. Hospital social workers are usually extremely knowledgeable about free or low-cost services that patients are eligible for and can receive at home. Mom's hospital social worker and nutritionist worked together and stopped the Meals on Wheels and got her connected with Manna. Manna is an agency that specializes in providing free nutritious gourmet meals to cancer patients. Mom had breakfast, lunch, and dinner delivered to her door every day for more than a year. Of course, Gracie didn't like the food, but I did. She also had the good-looking male hospice social worker as part of her team who was extremely helpful but in a different way. He made sure that Mom had the accommodations she needed at home to be comfortable, as part of her end-of-life care. He also helped me understand the benefits and limitations once a patient is in hospice.

**- Find out as much as you can about your loved one's health history and current symptoms while they remember.** Amnesia seems to kick in with some seniors when they're in the doctors' office. When the doctors asked Gracie a question she always said "I don't remember, ask her," as she sat quietly, pointing to me. That is until I misspoke; then she was quick to correct me.

**- Maintain an updated list of all of your loved one's medications.** Be prepared. At every doctor's appointment, someone will ask for a current list of your loved one's medications, including vitamin supplements.

**-Utilize technology when you can.** On most smart phones, there is a "Health App" where a loved one's health history, medication, and other vital health information can be stored. Having all of this in your phone is convenient and less cumbersome than carrying a notebook or folder. Only be sure to always carry your phone charger with you too.

**- Get an Advanced Directive and
discuss the DNR issue with your loved one.**
An Advanced Directive is how your loved one
legally appoints someone as their Medical Power of
Attorney and outlines their end of life healthcare
preferences in a DNR document. According to an
online article published by AARP, this process does
not require a lawyer but must be notarized and
have the signatures of one or two witnesses. DNR is
an abbreviation for Do Not Resuscitate. When a
patient is dealing with a terminal illness eventually,
the subject of end-of-life care will come up. The
person with the medical power of attorney has the
responsibility of insuring that the patients stated
preferences are followed. For example, one of the
questions on Mom's DNR form asked if the patient
is agreeable to a blood transfusion as a life-
preserving procedure. Gracie believed she
contracted hepatitis C from a blood transfusion
years earlier so she quickly answered "no" to that
question. As her power of attorney, it was my job to
make sure that no blood transfusions were done, but

rest assure she wanted everything else. In fact, she told me not to pull the plug on her unless I know for sure that she is "all the way dead."

**- Pay close attention when your loved one is reminiscing about their life.** Even when people are sick they may share good information that can be useful later. Because my Gracie-girl repeated her stories a lot, I was prepared for the often-daunting task of writing her eulogy.

**- Embrace the tears.** Many caregivers prefer to focus all of their attention on their sick loved one. They dismiss their own emotional needs, but grieving is inevitable. Caregivers may find themselves getting teary and feeling sad or angry for no apparent reason at inopportune times, even before their loved one dies. Instead of releasing their tears and talking about being over whelmed by the responsibilities and their emotional pain, many people choose to hold it all in. Although it may feel embarrassing or inconvenient, I believe it's better to have an emotional meltdown than a blow-up. Ask any grief counselor, it really is healthier for all involved including the caregiver, to release their grief before and after their loved one passes away.

Of course, this is not a complete list of what is needed to manage an ailing loved one's affairs. But being aware of just a few of these essential bits of information can help you remain calm and gracious as more needs arise. The administrative responsibilities were challenging, but I would do it all again and more for my Gracie-girl.

# seventeen

## Knowing Grace

In a conversation with a doctor friend, I learned that it is not unusual for some patients that have battled long-term debilitating illnesses, to know when it's their time to die. They may not know the exact day or hour but I believe by God's grace they are made aware of when its their general time to transition from this life to the next. I recall a dear friend sharing with me that before dying, her mother made telephone calls to several relatives and church members to say goodbye because she was going home to be with the Lord. Of course, this really freaked out my friend and she asked her mother to stop doing that. But her mother encouraged her to just accept the fact that her time here on Earth was over and now it's her time to go. Another close friend told me that just before her father passed away, he kept telling her and her siblings that he wanted to go home. In response, they started putting their heads together to figure out how they could take care of their dad's medical needs in the comfort of his family home where he raised his family. It was not until after the fact that she realized her dad was not talking about his physical house but his home in Heaven, where he could see his wife and son again. When my mother-in-law was hospitalized for ovarian cancer, I asked her to please hold on so she could see her son receive his bachelor's degree. She then asked me for his expected graduation date. When I told her that he will be graduating next spring semester (ten months later) she laughed and said " Girl you must be crazy! I'll be gone by then," and she was.

One morning, I had a very unexpected encounter with my Gracie-girl about a month before she passed away. As I was laying on the couch with the covers over my head hoping to delay the start of the day just a little longer, Mom came into the living room and says in a soft cheery voice "good morning" and opened the blinds. She didn't open the blinds completely, just enough so the bright, morning light could shine directly on my face as I peeked out from under the blanket. I should have known when I heard her rustling around in her bedroom that something was up. She was not one to sleep very late but she typically did not get out of the bed and start moving before 9 a.m. and it was only about seven o'clock.

When I took a sneak peek at her from under the blanket I could see that she was smiling. That should have been another clue that something out of the ordinary was about to happen. In my head, I wanted to tell her that I wasn't ready to get up yet. Before I could say anything she stood by the window and opened two of the blind slats even

101

wider with her hands and said, "it's my time." Of course, I immediately snatched the covers from over my head so I could get a good look at her and fully process what she was saying. She leaned toward the window. Her eyes were squinting as she faced the gap she made in the blinds and appeared to be looking up at the sky. Then she said it again: "it's my time." Turning to look directly at me, she nodded her head up and down and said, "yeah, you know what I'm talking about, it's my time." Satisfied that she got my attention and that I heard her grand announcement, she removed her hand from the blinds, stepped away from the window, retreated to her bedroom, got in the bed and went back to sleep. On the other side of the wall, I was now wide awake and I didn't know what to do with myself. Later that day I shared Mom's revelation with my sister, which left her speechless, too. I now know that Gracie letting me know what she knew to be true was a gift to help us mentally prepare for what was soon to come.

Approximately a week before her transition, she lost her ability to speak but her eyes were very expressive. Sometimes, I would see her laying in the bed smiling looking upward toward the ceiling across the room. Her eyes would be very wide like she was seeing something that was truly amazing. A few times, I got in the bed beside her and positioned myself just like her, looked up at the ceiling across the room but I saw absolutely nothing. I would ask her what she saw, but of course, there was no response. When Mom did take her last breath, I was comforted in believing that she saw a preview of where she was going when she left this life, and that it was good.

# eighteen

## Going with Grace

Once Mom made her announcement that it was "her time," it seemed as if the rate of her declining health accelerated. First, she started losing her physical strength and wasn't able to walk or feed herself. Then she stopped talking but she still smiled. When she had no desire to eat her mints or peach ice cream, I knew the end was near.

Sometimes, when one of my close friends gives me a weird response because they didn't clearly hear what I asked but respond anyway, teasingly

I say, "you know hearing is the first thing to go." While caring for my Gracie-girl, I learned from her nurse that hearing is actually the last of the senses to shut down.

On the day my mom passed away, I had a strong feeling we were at the end of her journey. I had a few important errands I needed to do, so the nurse's aide came to stay with her so I could go. Before leaving, I whispered in Mom's ear that I'd be back shortly and to wait for me. I specifically said, "don't leave here without me." By this time, she couldn't talk at all, but I was confident that she heard me.

Several months prior to this, I had a dream that my sisters and I were with our mother, sitting around her as she laid in the center of her queen size bed with her eyes closed. In the dream, we thought she died. While we wondered what to do, suddenly Gracie-girl opened her eyes. She informed us that the next time she sees Jesus, they are going to have fun.

Perhaps it was selfish of me to tell Mom not to leave without me. But I knew from the time I had that dream, that I definitely wanted to be with my Gracie-girl when she transitioned. Fortunately, by the grace of God, I was there and it felt like my older sister was there too. She happened to call my cell phone just as I realized our mother was literally dying in front of my eyes. I put the phone to Mom's ear so she could hear my sister express her last goodbyes. Then I held Mom's hand a little tighter and I told her that I loved her and it was okay to go and have fun with Jesus. Soon after that, she exhaled for the last time. On the evening of March 9th, 2017 Gracie peacefully transitioned from this life into the next. I was grateful to be there and hold her hand as she took her last breath. She was 85 years, 9 months and 11 days old. March 9th is also my son's birthday. I was not surprised that Gracie transitioned on a day that she knew I would never forget.

# nineteen

## A Touch of Grace

It is very interesting to me that someone can demonstrate little quirks all of their life that everyone notices but no one talks about until that person dies. My mom had the habit of sticking up her pinky finger when she drank from a cup. Most of her life she struggled financially, but when drinking her morning coffee, her pinky finger was always erect as if she embodied the persona of a queen. After Mom's funeral, I and other family members commented on how while laying in the coffin her pinky finger on her right hand was sticking up. I didn't know other people knew that about Gracie-girl, so it felt good to laugh about it at the repast. I concluded that it was her signal to us all that she was the matriarch of our family until the very end.

Her erect pinky finger also awakened a personal memory for me. Years ago, when I knew my marriage was crumbling, I tried to escape the pain by keeping busy and traveling as often as possible. Some of the travel was for work but there was also a lot for pleasure. On one particular occasion, I flew to Tampa, Florida, where my mom and I were meeting for a family reunion. This was after first visiting my sister in California and the two of us spending a few days in Las Vegas. Approximately 10 minutes prior to landing in Florida, thoughts about my failing relationship started rushing to my mind. In an effort to hide the tears and hold on to my sanity, I put on my happy face and shoved my marital problem to the back burners. After the family reunion meet-and-greet,

Mom and I agreed to hang out on the beach. Needless to say, my emotional pain and jet lag came along, too. I felt so drained that all I could do was lay on my back in the sun with my feet buried in the sand and let the waves from the ocean ride over me. Gracie was never one to pry into my personal business or ask too many tough questions. That day, she stayed true to form. She laid with me in the sun and sand for what seemed like hours. Neither of us said a word. Mom and I laid there quietly, side by side, just close enough so that our pinky fingers were barely touching.

We were on the beach until sunset. As my reality drifted to the forefront of my mind, my feet sunk deeper into the sand while quiet tears rolled down the sides of my face into the hollows of my ears. Mom never said a word; she just let her pinky finger get a little closer to mine. Her gentle touch was amazingly comforting.

While raising us, Gracie-girl was not the huggy kissy type of mother. But after her first breast

111

cancer diagnosis in 1998, she started telling my sisters and me, as well as her grandchildren, "I love you" before she would hang up the phone with us. She said this at the end of every phone conversation without fail, until the illness prohibited her from talking at all.

That summer afternoon having my mom lay beside me in the sand, and experiencing her support without judgment, was as soothing as being rocked in her arms. When I think about her funeral, I instantly remember her royal pinky pose. Which leads me to reflect on our time at the beach and my mom's same pinky finger gently attaching to mine. All I can say is, thank you for your touch, "Queen Grace."

# twenty

## Moments of Grace

It's been a year now since my mother has passed away. Not too many days go by when I don't think of her. I'll see a middle-aged woman helping an older woman shop or get in or out of a car, and remember when I was doing that with my Gracie-girl. Just the other day, I stood behind an older woman at the check out line in a local department store. She was having a serious senior moment. To get her bonus points for being a faithful customer, she needed to tell the cashier her phone number beginning with the area code: She could not recall the requested information even if her life depended on it. Like my Gracie-girl, she was an attractive woman. However, her inability to respond to the cashier was a dead giveaway for me that she was probably older than she appeared at first glance. I saw her frantically digging in her purse, then giving the cashier that deer-in-the-headlights look as if she had no clue as to what she was looking for or why. Other waiting customers got out of that line, but I couldn't move. I knew it was going to be a long wait while the cashier and the senior customer resolved this issue, but I was mesmerized. This beautiful, confused old lady reminded me of the days when Grandmom-Gracie would draw a blank when asked a simple question. Luckily for her, often I was there to quickly feed her the answer. Unfortunately, this senior lady appeared to be shopping alone. I attempted to assist, by telling her the most likely area code for this county but it didn't help. Completely frustrated, the cashier told her to just forget it for now and save her receipt so she can apply for her reward points online. I wanted to ask him "how likely do you think that's going to happen?"

Periodically I experience moments of déjà vu. But what is ever-present in my mind are the life lessons that I learned from my mother and some of the expressions she frequently said. After viewing the photos, you will find some of those "Gracie sayings" in Part 2. As promised, Part 3 provides space for you to document reflections and experiences from your own journey of grace.

*Photos*

Rev. Henderson Lester Sr.
Grace's maternal grandfather
1846 - DOD unknown

Hannah Strickland –Lester
Grace's maternal grandmother
DOB-DOD unknown

Gaddis Huff
Grace's father
1899 -1991

Ethel Lester-Huff
Grace's mother
1904 -1936

"Aunt Alice"
Alice Lester-Johnson
Grace's aunt
1895-1986

122

"Uncle Bobby"
Robert Johnson
Grace's uncle
DOB-DOD unknown

Grace on vacation in Nassau VI,
1975

Grace posing with the Michael Jackson
impersonator at Lester Family reunion
2014

Grace in her Sunday best with
Cousin Joey, (the MJ impersonator)
at the Lester Family  Reunion
2014

PART 2

*Expressions*

*&*

*Lessons of*

*Grace*

Whether it was one of her Gracie expressions that I've heard all of my life or something I watched her do, there are definitely unforgettable lessons that I learned from my mother. Here are ten of my most memorable:

### 1. "I'm the mother, you the child!"

Mom may have been saying this expression before I was born, but I remember hearing it most when I was a teenager. Like many teens, I secretly thought I knew more than adults, especially my mother. So, when I would give Gracie my unsolicited suggestions about what could be done about a situation, she would sternly say, "remember -- I'm the mother, you the child!"

During the last year before she passed away, I frequently asked the nurses aide to encourage Mom to drink water. To urge her to cooperate, one of them said, "Miss Grace your daughter really wants you to drink more water." Mom's response to her was, "you tell my daughter I'm still the mother and she's still the child".

### 2. "A hard head makes a soft behind."

My mother was a tough disciplinarian. She did not tolerate disrespect or disobedience from her children. However, when she saw us being stubborn or repeatedly making the same mistake, she would give us this warning "you know a hard head makes a soft behind." If the mistake or infraction happened again, you could rest assured that we had to face Gracie's wrath.

### 3. " If you're big enough to hit, you're big enough to get hit back."

As children, my siblings and I were taught to physically defend ourselves and one another but were highly discouraged from games that involved hitting each other although we did it anyway. If I complained to Mom that my brother hit me, she always asked if I hit him first or if we were playing a hitting game. After she asked those questions and gave me "the look," I'd just walk away so I wouldn't have to hear her lecture. On the other hand, that was also Gracie's position if a neighbor complained that one of us hit their child. No matter how young or small the other child was, my mom knew she raised us not to start fights or hit another child first. So, in our defense, her response was the same. "If your child is big enough to hit, they're big enough to get hit back."

### 4. "Don't tell nobody that!"

This is something Gracie would often say when she didn't believe me. I also think it was her way of trying to save me from embarrassment. In middle school, for some unknown reason, telling an unbelievable lie sounded better to me than admitting the truth.

I vividly remember when I was in the fifth grade Mom bought me a purse that I didn't like, so I traded it with a friend. When she asked me where my new purse was, instead of telling the truth, I made up an outrageous tall tale. With all of the seriousness a ten-year-old could muster, I told her that I wrapped the straps of the new purse around my right ankle then I turned to my left foot to tie my shoe and when I looked back at my right ankle, my new purse was gone and this purse was there in its place. After taking a few deep breaths (probably holding back her laughter) she grabbed me by the chin so I had to look directly into her eyes. She told me to go back to the place where this happened, put this purse around my right ankle, tie my shoe on my left foot and when I'm finished, the purse that she bought better be put back on my right ankle. After letting go of my chin, Gracie ended her lecture by saying, "and don't tell nobody else that!"

### *5. Lipstick makes you feel better.*

At some point – maybe during her last six months – my Gracie-girl decided that she couldn't leave her apartment, not even to check the mail, without putting on her lipstick. It is possible that I may be biased, but although Mom had lost a few pounds and was fighting for her life, she really didn't look sick until her last month or so. Regardless of her age and the chronic illness, I always tried to reassure her that she looked fine. Despite what I said, it was difficult getting her to leave on time for a doctor's appointment because at the last minute she insisted on going to the bathroom and standing in front of the mirror to put on her lipstick. When we were at risk of missing the para-transit ride and she could tell I was getting frustrated, she would say something like, "even though my body is sick, wearing lipstick makes me feel better." That response always worked to release the hot air swelling in my head.

### 6.  *"Read your Bible every day."*

For a Christmas gift in 2004 Mom gave me a "One Year Bible". The idea is to read the assigned scriptures each day and within one year you will have read the entire Bible. On a sticky note that she put on the inside of the front cover, she wrote:

"Read your bible every day, that's where your blessings come from." She also purchased a "One Year Bible" for herself. I will always cherish the memory of those mornings when she and I sat together in silence in her living room, reading the same Bible passages in preparation for the day ahead.

### 7. Pay your tithes.

Mom served as a trustee of her church for more than twenty years. After she was diagnosed with cancer for the second time, she relinquished her trustee position. During the 70's the Glory Baptist church was a vibrant congregation with many members. Over time the congregation dwindled, but they managed to pay off the mortgage for their church building. This is an accomplishment that the few remaining members, including Gracie, were very proud of. Regardless of whether her income source was from her salary or her Social Security check she considered it her duty to financially contribute to the church every month.

Mom mailed her tithes (ten percent of her income) to the church after she was no longer able to attend services in person. When her finances became my responsibility, she instructed me to write her tithes check first, even before paying her rent. During our conversations about giving, Gracie always said that she now had more of everything than she ever had in her entire life. She gladly declared that whatever she gave to the church was very little compared to all the blessings she received from the Lord.

### 8. *"It bees that way sometimes."*

The older Mom got, the more I heard her say this. It became Gracie's go-to-phrase when negative things happened. However, it really wasn't what she said but how she said it. Her voice was monotone and her facial expression would be very calm, almost expressionless. So, when she said "it bees that way sometimes," it always gave me the feeling that I/we had to accept the situation as it was but the disappointment would not last and I/we will survive. Maybe because I knew she had overcome her fair share of obstacles, her simplistic perspective of negative outcomes made some disappointments easier to bear.

### 9. With mints, it's all good.

Grabbing fists full of mints just before leaving home for doctor's appointments became another one of Gracie's rituals. In retrospect, I think having her pockets bulging with sweet treats may have helped Mom feel less nervous about her appointment. While waiting to be seen by the doctor, we sat in an area with other cancer patients. Unfortunately, the devastating effects of the disease and/or their treatments, were quite visible. Some patients wore a mask to protect their fragile immune system. Others looked very feeble, and some revealed significant hair loss. Gracie kept herself occupied by eating one mint after the other with her eyes focused on the TV. The positive side of her confectionary obsession was that when she had plenty of mints to eat, she did not complain about being hungry.

### *10. Life is short, enjoy it when you can.*

This is not something I remember her actually saying. But the older she got, it's a belief that I saw my Gracie-girl live.

## PART 3

*Your Journey*

*of*

*Grace Journal*

# Introduction

Initially, when I think about the characteristics associated with grace, I imagine a gentle, yet coercive energy, like the budding of a rose. Each phase of the blooming process has the power to draw us near as its sweet aroma and brilliant color is revealed. In like manner, throughout my life grace has gently drawn me back to a place of clarity and balance when I've been off kilter and I really do appreciate it. On the other hand, when frustration, disappointment or guilt seemed to hover over me like a dark cloud, I've experienced the strong presence of grace blaze through my fortress of insecurities like a superhero, rescue me from the trappings of negative thinking and simultaneously motivate me to trust and try again.

While reading my experiences with my Gracie-girl, as she transitioned from life to life, hopefully it has been clear that only by daily doses of God's grace, did I successfully managed the multiple responsibilities.

I believe that the form of grace we experience is determined by what we need. For example, accessing adequate resources is an ongoing issue for many, including me. In response to my need, grace has often manifested in my life as an invitation for an unexpected opportunity. At other times, grace has simply been the courage to ask for what I want, or a nudge of encouragement to maintain my faith as I wait for the blessing that is on the way.

As I reflect on my journey of grace there are a few things that I now know without a shadow of a doubt. First and foremost, with grace I know I can survive grief and loss. Also, with the confidence of grace, I always have hope and can live free from the deception of self-pity. Last but not least, because of grace I know that I don't have to be fearful of time; losing time, times past or whatever time I have in the future. With grace, time is on my side.

How about you? When have you received favor that you did not deserve and could not earn? Or found yourself extending kindness or choosing not to respond with vengeance when by all accounts it would be justified?

On the following pages share your journey of grace. Feel free to document your reflections related to loss or any life transition. Even if you think you are the only person who will ever read it, remember: reflecting on personal growth is self-nurturing and equally important is recognizing areas where more character development is needed.

Phrases have been provided to help you get started. While journaling, keep in mind that this exercise is most beneficial when you are honest and write from the heart. Also, there are no wrong answers even unpleasant memories can reveal life lessons learned. Always remember, regardless of what your life looks like, we have all been granted an accessible measure of grace.

*Because of grace ...*

_____

_____

_____

*Grieving is...*

_____

_____

_____

*One of my fondest memories is ...*

_____

_____

_____

*I wish I knew more about ...*

_____

_____

_____

*At certain times of the year I...*

*Forgiveness is ...*

_____

_____

_____

*I am looking forward to ...*

_____

_____

_____

*I smile when ...*

_____

_____

_____

*I am grateful for ...*

*I will always love ...*

_____

_____

_____

# References

1. www.merriam-websterdictionary.com
2. Smith, B. and Gasby, D.,(2016) Before I Forget. New York: Harmony Books
3. Signs and Symptoms of Sundowning Syndrome-WebMD. December 10,2017
4. Caring Tips for Creating Advance Directives. www.aarp.org
5. www.bizjournal.com.bartramvillage

Feel free to post comments on the "The Ways of Grace" Facebook page TWo-G@noblestrengthpublishing or send a message to the author at akharem@me.com.